Daphne du Maurier's
CORNWALL

DAPHNE DU MAURIER'S
CORNWALL

HER PICTORIAL MEMOIR

First published in 1995

Daphne du Maurier's Cornwall is edited, designed and produced by Piers Dudgeon for the Chichester Partnership. It is an abridged edition of *Enchanted Cornwall* by Daphne du Maurier, published in 1989 by Michael Joseph Ltd in association with Piers Dudgeon and now out of print. The majority of photographs are, however, quite new to the text and come from Dame Daphne's own collection, others from Piers Dudgeon, The National Maritime Museum, Redruth Library, and a number of landscape photographs taken by Christian Browning specifically for this book. Line maps are by Rob Shone. The painting of Jamaica Inn on page 31 is by Wilf Plowman.

Quotations from the following books by Daphne du Maurier by kind permission of Victor Gollancz Limited, London, and Doubleday Inc, New York:

The Loving Spirit	*Vanishing Cornwall*
Jamaica Inn	*The House on the Strand*
Rebecca	*Rule Britannia*
Frenchman's Creek	*Growing Pains*
The King's General	*The Rebecca Notebook*
My Cousin Rachel	*The Birds*
Castle Dor	

Typeset by J&L Composition, Filey, North Yorkshire
Printed by Tien Wah Press (PTE.) Limited, Singapore

Contents

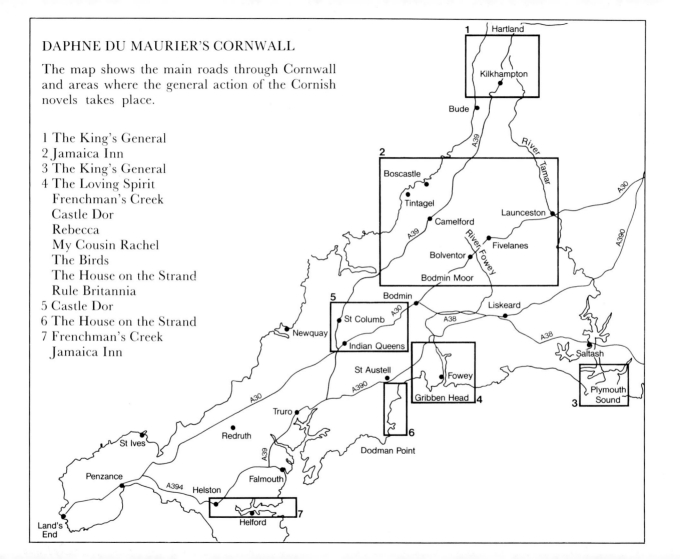

DAPHNE DU MAURIER'S CORNWALL

The map shows the main roads through Cornwall and areas where the general action of the Cornish novels takes place.

1 The King's General
2 Jamaica Inn
3 The King's General
4 The Loving Spirit
  Frenchman's Creek
  Castle Dor
  Rebecca
  My Cousin Rachel
  The Birds
  The House on the Strand
  Rule Britannia
5 Castle Dor
6 The House on the Strand
7 Frenchman's Creek
  Jamaica Inn

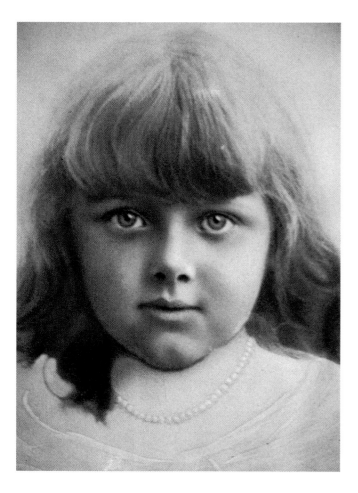

Foreword

Daphne du Maurier was born at 24 Cumberland Terrace, near Regents Park in London, on May 13th, 1907. Her father, Gerald, was the matinée idol of the day, creator of such action-packed theatrical roles as Raffles and Bulldog Drummond, characters perfectly in tune with the mood of the era. As actor-manager from 1917 of London's Wyndham's Theatre, he enjoyed a period of enormous success, bringing to West End audiences the work of such popular writers as Edgar Wallace and J M Barrie. Daphne's mother, Muriel Beaumont, also an actress, met Gerald in 1902, when they performed together at the Duke of York's in a play called 'The Admirable Crichton', written by J M Barrie.

Barrie himself, who captured the imaginations of millions of children by daring them to fly with him through the nursery window, was a permanent feature of Daphne's childhood. She knew him as Uncle Jim and Peter Pan was modelled on stories Barrie had made up for Daphne's own cousins, the five sons of Arthur and Sylvia Llewelyn Davies.

By her own account, she lived then in 'a world of make-believe and imagination,' the beguilingly alternative line of 'let's pretend' entering her life story from the very first page. She loved the theatre backstage, the

I was born into a world of make-believe and imagination.

'musty, indefinable smell of shifting scenery', the theatrical transformation of her actor father, the thrill and excitement of the star's dressing room, but most of all she loved those occasions when Gerald performed real magic on stage, as in his acclaimed portrayal of Will Dearth in Barrie's 'Dear Brutus'. She watched as he became 'every man who carries in his soul a seed of discontent, wishing that his world was other than it turned out to be'. It was a performance hinting at an imaginative purpose beyond the rattling good yarn, and Daphne, even as a child of ten, appreciated it as special.

The magical make-believe world of theatre and also books, which became her passion, was never less than real to Daphne, and in her teens the idea that imagination could turn an inner eye to truth was hungrily assimilated. She already knew that imagination created good fictions – Robert Louis Stevenson's *Treasure Island*, first read when she was 8, was her earliest favourite – but now she began to appreciate the purpose of imagination to enlighten too.

Dickens, George Eliot, the Brontës and Katherine Mansfield were among those who guided her through

It took James M Barrie to draw the finest acting out of the matinée idol of the day. 'Dear Brutus' saw Gerald du Maurier at his acting peak.

adolescence, and the work of her own grandfather, the famous illustrator and novelist, George du Maurier, whose imagination appeared to have broken the mortal barrier of time itself, made a particularly significant impact. 'My Grandpapa George developed the ability to "visit" the past by dreaming true,' she wrote. It was the central idea of his bestselling novel *Peter Ibbetson*, but it was also a real-life ability which would find echoes in Daphne's own experience.

Much later, the fast-developing science of genetics seemed to affirm what her imagination told her about the accessibility of the past. 'As an individual here and now I am only too aware that I possess feelings, emotions, a mind and body bequeathed to me by people long since dead . . . There is no cell in our bodies that has not been transmitted to us by our ancestors . . . We are all of us chemical particles, inherited not only from our parents but from a million ancestors. For this reason alone none of us is isolated in time, a mere expression of the present. In a very real sense, "yesterday is within us". We are part of what we were once and of what we are yet to become in successive generations.'

In her late teens, as she developed an imaginative

I was never myself in those days. I was whatever character that I was reading.

CHAPTER ONE

Gateway to Another World

inner life of her own, Daphne felt a need to escape her family. There was nothing antagonistic in this. She believed that any child destined to become a writer 'needs to escape the atmosphere around him, no matter how stable, even loving.' The theatre of her London childhood had been dreamt up by someone else, she wanted 'no ties, no binding chains,' save those she would forge for herself.

Cornwall offered the escape she craved, and met the challenge of her developing imagination in creative fashion. Other parts of England may be scarred with exploits of the past and sanctified in legend, other ancient buildings cobwebbed with what-has-been, but Cornwall offered her its singular text. Here Daphne found 'a sense of timelessness barely glimpsed before, a sense of continuity with ancient times, and more than this, a present which resonates with past and future – a sense indeed that past, present and future are not isolated milestones in time, to be feared, longed for, and finally met, but that they are one, each part of a whole, existing side-by-side.'

The stories conceived out of their inspired union were brewed in her imagination but to this day remain firmly rooted in the enchanted landscape to which she first came with her mother and two sisters, Angela and Jeanne, on September 13th, 1926.

Piers Dudgeon, 1995

The hired car swept round the curve of the hill, and suddenly the full expanse of Fowey harbour was spread beneath us. The contrast between this sheet of wide water, the nearby jetties, the moored ships, the grey roofs of Fowey across the way, the clustering cottages of Polruan on the opposite hill by the harbour mouth, and narrow, claustrophobic Looe where we had spent the night on our way down from London was astonishing, like the gateway to another world.

My spirits soared.

The car deposited my mother, Angela, me and Jeanne at the foot of the hill by the ferry. We could either cross the ferry to Fowey or lunch first at the Ferry Inn here in Bodinnick. It was nearly one o'clock, and we chose the latter course. Before climbing the hill to lunch our eyes were caught by a board saying 'For Sale' on a gate just above the ferry. Behind the gate was a rough piece of ground and a house just by the water's edge, a strange looking house, built like a Swiss chalet. 'Yes,' said the ferryman standing near by, 'they call it Swiss Cottage. They used to build boats there, down under, and have the second floor for lofts. The top floor was for living. It's for sale right enough,'

We went to the inn for lunch and afterwards during coffee, our mother talked with the proprietor, enquiring first about lodgings on the opposite side in Fowey

(pronounced Foy). We were touring Cornwall, she explained, with the idea of looking for a house in the holidays; we came from Hampstead, London . . .

I was too impatient to wait for the conversation to drag on. I jerked my head to the others to follow me, leaving my mother talking. We went down the hill. My sisters tried the gate by the ferry and went into the yard. I found another gate, and a pathway leading to the other side of the house. Here there was a garden, or what went for a garden, terraced uphill, tier upon tier, and the chalet part of the house thrust itself forward, built, so it seemed, against the rock, with the windows facing straight out across the harbour. I went and stood beneath the chalet, the water immediately beneath me, and looked towards the harbour mouth. There were small boats everywhere, and yachts at anchor, but more stirring still a big ship was drawing near, with two attendant tugs, to moor a few cables' length from the house itself. There was a smell in the air of tar and rope and rusted chain, a smell of tidal water. Down harbour, around the point, was open sea.

Here was the freedom I desired, long sought-for, not yet known. Freedom to write, to walk, to wander, free-

The hired car swept round the curve of the hill, and suddenly the full expanse of Fowey harbour was spread beneath us.

'They call it Swiss Cottage,' said the ferryman. 'They used to build boats there, down under, and have the second floor for lofts. The top floor was for living. It's for sale.'

Oh the happiness of those first weeks! The thrill of crossing backwards and forwards on the ferry never palled.

dom to climb hills, to pull a boat, to be alone. One feature of my excitement was the feeling that it could not be mere chance alone that brought us to the ferry. It seemed so right.

Swiss Cottage was bought and re-named Ferryside. Throughout winter and spring it was put in the hands of decorators and builders, and on May 14th, 1927, the day after my twentieth birthday, my mother and Angela, who had come with me to see the transformation, returned to London, leaving me on my own for the first time in my life.

Oh, the happiness of those first weeks! The thrill of crossing backwards and forwards on the ferry never palled. To stand on the Fowey side, at Passage slip, and shout 'Over!', and after a moment or two to see the cheery wave from the ferry man at Bodinnick, or better still, if a cart had to be transported, to cry, 'Horse-boat!' – none of your car ferries more than half-a-century ago.

Everyone in the village was so friendly. I soon got to know their names. The Swigges, the Couches, the Bunneys, the Hunkins up the road, little Miss Roberts waving from her cottage, her macaw, Robert, calling, 'Rob, Rob!' from the sea wall, old Captain Bate from across the harbour, who lent me a book called *Gypsy of the Horn* in which he had figured as the skipper.

I would awake of a morning and go to the window, and stare out across the harbour. Another ship had come to anchor during the night – what was her name? Where was she from? Fowey has always been a terrific port for the china clay trade – ships come from all over the world to load up at the jetties, and I became friendly with many of the seamen, drinking tea with them, listening to their stories. I remember one ship in particular, the Wearbridge, I would call out and wave to the skipper, Captain Richie Bird (Dickie Bird!), when the Wearbridge passed my window at Ferryside, and he would give a terrific hoot in return.

Then of course there was Adams, a veteran of Jutland, who taught me how to steer a boat in rough sea and not go on the rocks, and how to take a hook out of a fish's mouth without squirming. We would fish for conger-eel up by the jetties after dark, and go rabbiting together when winter came.

One day, on one of my walks up Pont Creek, an estuary of the Fowey which separates the two villages of Bodinnick and Polruan, I came upon a derelict schooner, called 'Jane Slade'. She lay there on the mud flats, abandoned to die, her hulk rotting but her colourful figurehead proudly challenging the passage of time. I used to visit her often, climbing aboard and imagining what seas she had once travelled, what her history had

Down harbour, around the point, was open sea. Here was the freedom I desired, freedom to write, to walk, to wander, freedom to climb hills, to pull a boat, to be alone.

been, who the men were that had manned her, now all dead and gone . . .

I asked Adams about the schooner and discovered that the figurehead was the carving of a real woman. Jane Slade had been the mother of the men who built the vessel at the boatyard at Polruan. What's more, Adams told me that his wife had been a Slade, a grand-daughter of the original Jane. 'There are stacks of old letters in a box,' he went on, 'all about the family, and when the Schooner was built. We'll look at them one day.' Some time later he took me to meet the man that then owned the Polruan boatyard, one Ernie Slade. Not only had Jane been his gran, but his uncle Tom was the old schooner's skipper and the hulk itself was at last to be broken up. 'Would you like to have the figurehead?'

And so the colourful carving came to rest on the beam outside my bedroom window at Ferryside. My interest in the family took me up to Lanteglos churchyard, high above the creek, to find where Jane had been buried, and sure enough there was the family tombstone – Christopher Slade and his wife Jane Symons, died 1885, aged seventy-two. Then Adams came along with his big box of letters and papers about the family, and I went

'The Janet Coombe [the Jane Slade] was to be carvel-built and the length of her was ninety-seven feet.' *The Loving Spirit*

The figurehead was the carving of Jane Slade (Janet Coombe), the mother of the men who built the vessel. 'Janet would know nothing of it until the day of the launching.'

through them that very same evening, faded handwriting, going back to the early part of the nineteenth century. They had about them a personal touch; it was almost as though I had opened up a coffin and looked upon the dead.

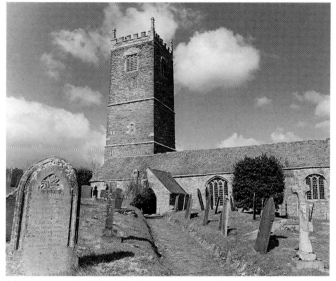

My interest in the Slade family took me up to Lanteglos churchyard to find where Jane had been buried, and sure enough there was the tombstone.

The following day I couldn't get them out of my head. I realised that there was enough material here for a book. The family Slade would become the Coombe family – Jane Slade, Janet Coombe – and Polruan would be re-named Plyn. Ernie Slade supplied more information, and soon I was busy drawing out a genealogical table of the whole family down to the present day. Was it my fancy, or was it true that Jane dominated them all, even after death? – and she would be getting on when the schooner was built . . . Poems and short stories were pushed aside, I could think of nothing but Jane Slade.

Then one night when the novel was still in embryo, scarcely born in thought, I walked up to Castle Point. The moon was high in the sky, and there was no sound but the moan of the still water lapping the rocks beyond the harbour. It seemed to me that I was standing on the cliffs years hence with a grown-up son. I was a ghost, long dead, existing only in his thoughts.

Janet leant against the castle ruins with the sea at her feet, and the light of the moon on her face. Then she closed her eyes, and the jumbled thoughts fled from her mind, her tired body seemed to slip away from her, and she was possessed with the strange power and clarity of the moon itself. When she opened her eyes for a moment there was a mist about her, and when it dissolved she saw kneeling beside the cliff with his head bowed in his hands, the figure of a man. She knew that he was filled with wild despair and bitterness, and that his poor lost soul was calling to her for comfort.

She went and knelt beside him, and held his head to her breast, while she stroked his grey hair with her hand.

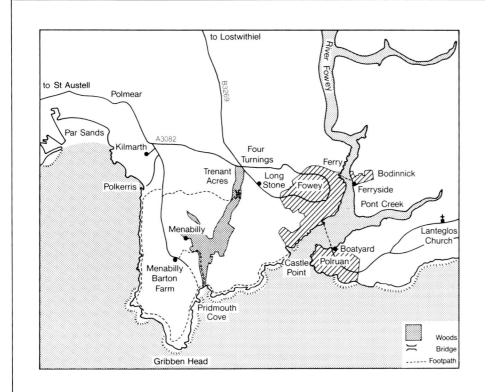

▨	Woods
≍	Bridge
-----	Footpath

The map shows Ferryside, Bodinnick, where Daphne wrote her first novel, The Loving Spirit; *Pont Creek, where the schooner, the Jane Slade, lay waiting for her to immortalise it in that novel; Lanteglos Church, where the Slades graves can still be seen, and where Dame Daphne was married; the Slades boatyard at Polruan (Plyn in the novel); and Castle Point, where the novelist found her inspiration.*

But the area is also the heart of du Maurier country, and includes important sites not only in The Loving Spirit, *but in* Rebecca, Frenchman's Creek, Castle Dor, My Cousin Rachel, The Birds, The House on the Strand *and* Rule Britannia. *The recommended footpath, largely coastal, takes in many of the sites referred to in this book.*

Then he looked up at her, his wild brown eyes crazy with fear at himself. And she knew him to belong to the future, when she was dead and in her grave, but she recognised him as her own . . .

'They've been long weary days since you went from me, an' I've not heeded your council, nor deserved your trust in me,' he told her. 'See how I'm old now, with the grey hairs in my head and beard, and you younger than I ever knew you, with your pale girl's face and your tender unworn hands.'

'I have no reckoning in my mind of what is past, nor that which is to be,' said she, 'but all I know is there's no space of time here, nor in our world, nor in any world hereafter. There be no separation for us, no beginnin' and no end – we'm cleft together you an' I, like the stars to the sky . . .'

He threw back his head and watched her as she stood, white against the sky with a smile on her lips.

'You're an angel tonight, ' he said, 'standing at the gates of Heaven before the birth of Christ . . .'

'Fifty years or a thousand years, it's all the same, ' said Janet. 'Our coming here together is the proof of it.'

'You'll never leave me again, then?' he asked.

'Never no more.'

He knelt and kissed her foot-prints in the snow.

Time and again Janet climbs to Castle Point. It seemed that this hillside was our own world, hers and mine, a small planet of strange clarity and understanding.

'Tell me, is there a God?'
He looked into her eyes and read the truth.
*They stood for a minute and gazed at each other, seeing themselves
as they never would on earth. She saw a man, bent and worn, with
wild unkempt hair and weary eyes; he saw a girl, young and fearless,
with the moonlight on her face.*
'Goodnight, my mother, my beauty, my sweet.'
'Goodnight, my love, my baby, my son.'
Then the mist came between them, and hid them from one another.

I began the novel, my first, on a terrible wild day in
October with a howling sou'westerly wind and slashing
rain, a rug wrapped round my knees, sitting at the desk
in my bedroom at Ferryside. It's title, *The Loving Spirit*,
came from a poem by Emily Brontë.

The discovery of the schooner and research into the
family that built her gave me the story, but my interest in
the Slade family was really only the vehicle for what had
at last made me sit down and write a full-length work.
The inspiration to write a novel comes from within. *The
Loving Spirit* was inspired by the sense of freedom that
my new existence at Ferryside brought.

Time and again in the story Janet climbs to Castle
Point to be 'nearer to something to which there was no
name.' Here, 'things have no reckoning of time.' It
seemed that this hillside was our own world, hers and

mine, a small planet of strange clarity and understanding. There was a freedom here, a freedom that was part of the air and the sea; like the glad tossing of the leaves in autumn, and the shy fluttering wings of a bird.

Janet longs for freedom as I had longed for it; a throb of intense pain would shake her being when she saw a ship leave the harbour of Plyn, her sails spread to the

wind, moving away like a silent phantom across the face of the sea. Something would tear at her heart to be gone too, to be part of the ship, part of the seas and the sky above, with the glad free ways of the gull.

I can't remember exactly how well *The Loving Spirit* sold, but after its publication I had my independence. I could come down to Fowey when I liked, do what I liked and pay for myself. The driving force was that I must be free. The one led to the other, just as, in the end, Joseph would give Janet her freedom too:

It was close to sunset, and the tide had made its highest mark. The red light of the sky glittered upon the houses, and the parting smile of the sun lingered upon the water. All Plyn was gathered about the slip to watch the ship lunge into the sea. The yard was decorated with flags, and thronged with folk. A chair had been brought for Janet, and she was seated upon it, her hand on Joseph's arm. Her eyes were on the figurehead of the ship. It was Janet herself, Janet with her dark hair and eyes and her firm chin; dressed in white with her hand at her breast . . .

She heard none of the cheers; in her ears were the call of the wind and the cry of the waves. Beyond the hill the sun glimmered for an

Slades Shipbuilding Yard, Polruan. 1887. Seated farthest right, middle row, is Joseph Slade of *The Loving Spirit*.

instant – a ball of fire. A great shout arose from the people: 'There she goes!' The harbour rang with their cries and the mighty crash as the vessel struck the water. At the sound a shudder passed through Janet's body and she opened her arms. Her eyes were filled with a great beauty, like the light of a star, and her soul passed away into the breathing, living ship.

CHAPTER TWO
Old, Unhappy, Far-off Things

The sea helped form the Cornish character. Their ancestors were probably immigrant merchants from Mediterranean lands, who sailed the seas in search of riches, and came upon Cornwall by luck or accident.

The sea is itself a symbol of the uncertainties of fate. 'You will embark on a fair sea, and at times there will be fair weather and foul,' said the priest at my wedding day at Lanteglos church. 'Never lose courage. Safe harbour awaits you both in the end.' The imagery was so typical of a Cornishman responsible for the souls of a village whose people depended for centuries on the sea.

The Cornish fisherman confronts almost daily the uncertainties of the elements, the wilfulness of Fortune with faith and skills accumulated over centuries of experience. That many a fisherman has been drowned and his boat smashed is due, not to ignorance but to the daring and courage flowing in his blood. Wise in the weather, he knows that when the wind backs with the changing of the tide there could be increase in wind and sea, and the smallest miscalculation in the timing of his return to harbour might spell danger, even disaster; but the desire to bring home a full catch and beat the weather will win over prudence every time. Down the years the heroic uncertainties of his ancient trade came to permeate the life of the coastal community, drawing

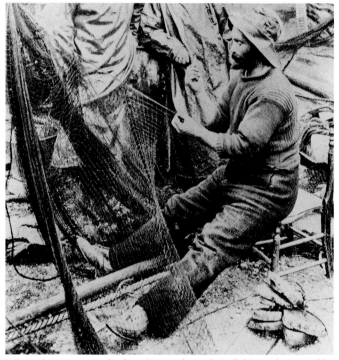

When the men came back to Fowey from their fishing, they would lean over the wall by the slip and gossip over their pipes, the nets spread out to dry on the cobbled stones.

men, women and children into an activity central to their lives.

A Frenchman, one Alphonse Esquiros who ventured to Cornwall in the nineteenth century, was impressed by the stoicism of the Cornish in the face of great hardship and poverty, but he sought in vain for the scenes of domestic joy and happiness so sweetly described by English poets. The peasants, he found, spoke little, and it was difficult to discover the reason for this silence which at times resembled coldness. Was it indifference to their mode of life? Was it resignation, of that species of tacit contentment which the consciousness of a strict duty accomplished imparted to a man?

In truth it was none of these. The reserve which Monsieur Esquiros observed in the Cornish character was something sturdier, more deep-rooted, a self-sufficiency bred in the bone through centuries of independence and being largely his own master, with a natural scepticism and suspicion of the stranger who asked questions.

Take the tinners, they were at work among the rocks and furze of Cornwall back in the Bronze Age, some 1800 years BC, though it was not until the fifteenth century AD that they began to mine beneath the surface. The tinners became an essential part of Cornwall – hunters, seekers – spending themselves in the unending quest for 'treasure' underground. They were a race of individualists, making their own terms wherever they streamed or dug for tin, beset by no ring of employers as in other industries. They had a single-minded preference for an ancient occupation that entailed great courage and endurance. And it was in their individualism, as much as their own customs and pastimes (such as cock-fighting, wrestling, and hurling, which may sometimes have led to excess, drunkenness and bloody fights), that made them feared and frowned upon by outsiders.

In the mid-nineteenth century, tin and copper mining boomed in Cornwall in line with the advancements in engineering, transport and trade of the Industrial Revolution, and the county became the single largest copper producing district in the world, responsible for two-thirds of the entire world-wide supply. The boom peaked in the 1860s; copper had been found in Lake Victoria, tin in Malaysia. Foreign competition pricked the bubble, and before the end of the century one third of the mining population of Cornwall had taken their skills to other continents.

The collapse of the industry meant terrible destitution for some. From this period came stories of the tinners as a race of violent men who would stop at nothing, waylay travellers by night and beat them senseless, raid farms, set wrecking parties upon the cliffs with lanterns to lure

ships to their doom and plunder them. Such stories were founded on a reality of near starvation.

Many tinners who stayed after the collapse of their industry turned to china-clay, now Cornwall's greatest industry, its mines stretching across a high plateau encompassing White Moor and Hensbarrow Downs, outwards to Luxulyan and St Austell, west to Goss Moor and Indian Queens. Incredibly there are people today who object to the 'scars' that the clay industry has left upon the landscape. I think that the huge spoil heaps, with their attendant lakes, are absolutely beautiful and get livid when people suggest sowing grass seeds on them.

Smuggling came easy to a people who had deployed themselves in piracy during the fifteenth and sixteenth centuries – a legacy of the 100 Years' War when the Cornish provided transport ships to carry Plantagenet armies across the Channel. The owners of these ships found it profitable to attack and board a French vessel, subdue her crew, loot her contents and either sink her or bring her home as a prize. Following the end of the war, the taste remained, eventually to be replaced by smuggling.

The hey-day of smuggling occurred during the nineteenth century when the Industrial Revolution was upsetting the old tenor of life, fortunes were being made or lost in tin and copper, and society was changing into the 'haves' and 'have-nots'.

Although not all smugglers were needy, smuggling was at root a product of severe economic conditions – the exhaustion of tin seams, even the seasonal patterns of fishing. The transgression of the law which it undoubtedly involved, was justified in many a Cornishman's mind by a deeper sense of justice than society's which condemned him to hardship and poverty. You could be a smuggler and yet an honest man in all your dealings; smuggling – or fair trading, as it was called – smacked of the heroic, and tales of smuggling took their place among the myths and legends which lie deep in the Cornish psyche.

But if smuggling was largely the result of poverty, it also appealed to the better off as an extremely profitable business. Quite simply, everybody benefited from smuggling. The tinner down on his luck, the Squire who liked his brandy, the Squire's lady who dressed in lace, even the vicar of the parish – often a relation of the Squire – each participated in his own fashion, and the necessity of sharing hazards made a link between all parties.

Incredibly there are people today who object to the 'scars' that the clay industry has left. Theirs is a strange, almost fantastic beauty . . . like another world.

The hey-day of smuggling was the 19th century. A boat would pull into any one of the hundreds of suitable inlets. In the pretty fishing village of Helford, seen here, when there was talk of smuggling, it was with a wink and a smile of indulgence.

A boat would pull into any one of the hundreds of suitable inlets around the Cornish coast and the cargo stored – not necessarily in the inevitable cave of romance and legend but often in the homes or storerooms of obliging persons nearby, frequently merchants who had access to waggons, or neighbouring farmers, or even the local Squire with suitable cellars. Then the contraband would be moved across the country often at night by waggons led by horses with muffled hoofs, and it might be secreted away on the lonely moors before final dispersal.

Mary listened, hearing nothing at first but the thumping of her own heart, but in a few minutes there came another sound, from beneath her room this time – the sound of heavy things being dragged along the stone flags in the passage downstairs, bumping against the walls.

She got out of bed and went to the window, pulling aside an inch of blind. Five waggons were drawn up in the yard outside. Three were covered, each drawn by a pair of horses, and the ramaining two were open farm-carts. One of the covered waggons stood directly beneath the porch, and the horses were steaming . . .

She began to understand. Packages were brought by the waggons and unloaded at Jamaica Inn. They were stored in a locked room. The horses were steaming because they had come over a great distance – from the coast perhaps – and as soon as the waggons were unloaded they would take their departure, passing out into the night as swiftly and as silently as they had come.

Joss Merlyn came out of the porch, the pedlar at his side. Neither wore coat or hat, in spite of the cold air, and both had sleeves rolled to the elbows. 'Is that the lot?' the landlord called softly, and the driver of the last waggon nodded, and held up his hand. The men began to climb into the carts . . .

The Haven, in Fowey, home of Sir Arthur Quiller-Couch. Our friendship began when I was invited one Sunday to tea.

So the waggons and the carts departed from Jamaica, creaking out of the yard, one after the other in a strange funeral procession, some turning north and some south when they came out on to the high road, until they had all gone, and there was no one left standing in the yard but one man Mary had not seen before, the pedlar, and the landlord of Jamaica Inn himself.

I owe my first sight of Jamaica Inn to a suggestion by Sir Arthur Quiller-Couch about a year after I had completed *The Loving Spirit*. Son of a Cornish doctor, Sir Arthur, or 'Q' as he was known to countless of his readers, was an important literary figure. Perhaps most famous as editor of the first *Oxford Book of English Verse*, he had been knighted in 1910 and two years later was appointed to the chair of English at Cambridge. Our friendship began when I was invited one Sunday to tea at his home, The Haven, in Fowey. Then, in November 1930, Q suggested that his daughter, Foy, and I should take a couple of horses and make an expedition to Bodmin Moor, putting up at the wayside hostelry.

Bodmin is the greatest and wildest stretch of moorland in Cornwall. Like Mary Yellan who, in the novel, comes to Bodmin Moor from the tranquil hills and valleys of Helford, I came unprepared for its dark, diabolic beauty. People say that my fictional characters seem to emerge from the places where my stories are set, and certainly when I first set eyes on the old, granite-faced inn itself it made me think that there was a story there, peopled

Brown Willy, Bodmin Moor. 'It was a silent, desolate country . . . vast and untouched by human hand; on the high tors the slabs of stone leant against one another in strange shapes and forms, massive sentinels who had stood there since the hand of God first fashioned them.' Jamaica Inn

with moorland folk in strange harmony with their background.

On the first afternoon following our arrival, Foy and I
experienced first-hand the despondency and near-panic
that Mary felt upon her first treck across the moor. We
had set out on horseback with the happy intention of
calling on an elderly lady living at Trebartha Hall about
five miles east of the inn. Surely, we told ourselves, it
would be no more than forty minutes ride at most.
Irresponsible, we trotted off across the moor no later
than two o'clock . . .

It was a cold grey day in late November. The weather had changed
overnight, when a backing wind brought a granite sky and a mizzling
rain with it, and although it was now only a little after two o'clock in
the afternoon the pallor of a winter evening seemed to have closed
upon the hills, cloaking them in mist. It would be dark by four.

After an hour or more we were little nearer to our
destination. Tors and boulders, inaccessible on horseback, even perhaps on foot, barred our passage. The
track leading us on descended to a slippery path that
disappeared, while beneath us a battered gate, swinging
by the hinges, gave access to a swollen stream. The day
comparatively fine until that moment, darkened, and a
black cloud, trailing ribbons, hovered above our head
and burst.

In a moment all was desolation. The ominous stream
rushed by with greater swiftness, turning to a torrent.
Forcing the horses up a steep incline, we plunged
onward, seeking escape. A deserted cottage, humped
beneath a hill, seemed our only hope – at least it would
be temporary refuge until the cloudburst ceased. We

rode towards it, dismounted, and led our horses to the rear. The cottage was not only empty but part fallen, with rain driving through the empty windows, and what roof there was had been repaired with corrugated tin, so that the cascading rain sounded like hailstones on its surface. We leant against the fungoid walls and brooded, Trebartha Hall a hundred miles away, Jamaica Inn an equal distance, and all the while the rain fell upon the corrugated roof to echo in a splashing water-butt nearby. I had never known greater despondency.

The wind tore at the roof, and the showers of rain, increasing in violence now there was no shelter from the hills, spat against the windows with new venom . . . The country stretched interminably into space. No trees, no lanes . . . mile upon mile of bleak moorland, dark and untraversed, rolling like a desert land to some unseen horizon.

It rained for a full hour, then turned to drizzle and dank fog, by which time our world was murky and we had lost all sense of compass points. Emerging from the ruins my companion, a better horsewoman than I and owner of both our steeds, looked about her and observed, 'There's nothing for it but to get into the saddle, leave our reins loose on their necks, and let them lead us home.'

I was not impressed by her suggestion, for where was home to the horses – thirty miles or more to Fowey, or back across the moors to Jamaica Inn? We mounted once again, darkness and silence all about us, save for that dreary patter on the cottage roof, and somewhere to our right the hissing storm.

The horses, sure footed even amongst dead heather and loose stones, plodded forward without hesitation, and there was some relief at last to be away from the abandoned cottage and in the open, however desolate, for there had been no warmth within its walls, no memories of hearths glowing with turf fire kindled by owners in the past. Surely whoever lived there before he let it fall to ruins had been sullen and morose, plagued by the Withey Brook that ran somewhere below his door, and in despair went out one night and drowned himself.

No human being could live in this wasted country, thought Mary, and remain like other people; the very children would be born twisted, like the blackened shrubs of broom, bent by the force of a wind that never ceased . . . Their minds would be twisted, too, their thoughts evil, dwelling as they must amidst marshland and granite, harsh heather and crumbling stone.

I suggested this to my fellow-traveller, who was not amused . . . Gaining higher ground we found ourselves facing a new hazard in the form of what appeared to be a disused railway track, upon which our mounts slithered and stumbled. A railroad in mid-moor. It could not be. Unless we had both gone mad and this was fantasy.

'A line for trolleys,' said my companion, 'leading to a stone-quarry. If the horses take us there they'll break their legs. Better dismount.' Bogs, quarries, brooks, boulders, hell on every side, we led the horses from the slippery track, and then got up on our saddles once again . . .

The horses, bolder now they were clear of the trolley-lines, headed steadily forward, straight across the moor, possibly in the direction of those menacing crags that we had seen in early afternoon, pointing dark fingers to the sky, which, we knew very well, lay contrary to any path for home.

It was seven, it was nine, it was midnight – too dark to see our watches, and fumbling fingers could not strike damp matches. On, forever on, nothing on all sides but waste and moor.

Suddenly my companion cried, 'They've done it . . . they've done it . . . Isn't that the road?'

Peering into the darkness ahead I saw a break in the rising ground, a new flatness, and there, not a hundred yards distant, the blessed streaky wetness of the Launceston-Bodmin road, and surprisingly, unbelievably, the gaunt chimneys of Jamaica Inn itself.

Mary stood alone, with the trunk at her feet. She heard a sound of bolts being drawn in the dark house behind her, and the door was flung open. A great figure strode into the yard, swinging a lantern from side to side.

'Who is it?' came the shout. 'What do you want here?'

Mary stepped forward and peered up into the man's face.

The light shone in her eyes, and she could see nothing. He swung the lantern to and fro before her, and suddenly he laughed and took hold of her arm, pulling her roughly inside the porch.

'Oh, it's you, is it?' he said. 'So you've come to us after all? I'm your uncle, Joss Merlyn, and I bid you welcome to Jamaica Inn.' He drew her into the shelter of the house, laughing again, and shut the door, and stood the lantern upon a table in the passage. And they looked upon each other face to face.

Today all is changed at the inn itself. Coaches, cars, electricity, a bar, dinner of river-trout, baths for the travel-stained instead of the cream-jug of hot water that we were offered. But if, when you go there, you wonder whether the novel was pure fancy, take a walk behind Jamaica and, one morning before sunrise, climb Rough Tor and listen to the wind in the stones. These moors have a fascination unlike any other, they are a survival from another age. They were the first things to be created; afterwards came the forests and the valleys and the sea. Nothing has really changed since Mary Yellan walked the moors, climbed the tors, and rested in the low dips beside the springs and streams.

Strange winds blew from nowhere; they crept along the surface of the grass, and the grass shivered; they breathed upon the little pools of rain in the hollowed stones, and the pools rippled. Sometimes the wind shouted and cried, and the cry echoed in the crevices, and moaned, and was lost again. There was a silence on the tors that belonged to another age; an age that is past and vanished as though it had never been, an age when man did not exist, but pagan footsteps trod upon the hills. And there was a stillness in the air, and a stranger, older peace, that was not the peace of God.

In the late summer of 1931, or it might have been in the early autumn, a thirty-five-year-old major in the Grenadier Guards, Boy Browning to his fellow officers, second-in-command to the second batallion of his regiment, said to one of his closest friends, 'I've read a novel called *The Loving Spirit*, one of the best books I've read for years, and apparently it's all about Fowey in Cornwall. I'm

Climb Rough Tor and listen to the wind in the stones: 'Sometimes the wind shouted and cried, and the cry echoed in the crevices, and moaned, and was lost again . . . there was a stillness in the air and a stranger, older peace, that was not the peace of God.' *Jamaica Inn*

determined to go down there in my boat Ygdrasil, and see the place for myself. Perhaps I'll have the luck to meet the girl who has written it. How about it? Will you come with me?' John Prescott, the brother-officer, agreed, and together they proceeded down the coast and arrived at Fowey. It was sister Angela who first spotted them.

'There's a most attractive man going up and down the harbour in a white motor-boat,' she said, watching through field-glasses from the hatch window at Ferryside. 'Do come and look.'

Mildly interested, I obeyed the summons. 'H'm,' I said, 'he is rather good.'

The cruising up and down continued through the weeks, and some local gossip informed us that the stunning helmsman was called Browning, and he was said to be the youngest major in the Brirish army! And that was that. I thought no more about him.

It was not until the following year, 1932, in April, having survived a mild operation for appendicitis, and arriving down in my beloved Fowey to recuperate, that I heard 'Major Browning' was in the harbour and afloat again, having laid-up his boat Ygdrasil with the Bodinnick boat-builder, one of my neighbours, George Hunkin.

Mrs Hunkin was my informant. 'The Major would like to meet you,' she told me, 'he's very nice.'

'Oh?'

The following day a note was brought to me by Mrs Hunkin, which, though alas I never kept it, read as follows, to the best of my belief, 'Dear Miss du Maurier, I believe my late father, Freddie Browning, used to know yours, as fellow-members of the Garrick Club. The Hunkins tell me you have had your appendix out and can't do much rowing yet, so I wonderd if you would care to come out in my boat? How about tomorrow afternoon?' I sent word back that I should be delighted.

Friday, April 8th. 'A fine bright day with a cold wind. In the afternoon I went out with Browning in his boat. It was the most terrific fun, the seas short and jumpy, and he put his boat hard into it, and we got drenched with spray. She's called Ygdrasil because he's mad on Norse mythology, and it means The Tree of Fate . . .'

The Tree of Fate . . . The next two days we spent entirely in each other's company, then he had to return to his batallion, but in a week he was back again, having driven through the night! I was sawing up some logs early in the morning, and I heard him call to the dog.

'There's a most attractive man going up and down the harbour in a white motor-boat,' she said, watching through the field- glasses from the hatch window.

My diary reads: 'His friends call him Boy, but he told me to call him Tommy, which is what his family call him . . . I feel I've known him for years.'

Hatless, brown leather jerkin, grey flannel trousers thrust into sea boots . . . green eyes and a smile that curled at one corner. Yes, no doubt about it, he was good . . .

So a rapid courtship began, and within a few weeks he became as wedded to Fowey – the harbour, the river, the walks, the people – as I was myself. By the end of June, after frequent visits, we decided to become engaged.

The sun shone for us on the day – July 19th – that we were married. At 8.15 am – time to catch the tide – my parents and I proceeded in our boat up Pont Creek to Lanteglos, Tommy and the Hunkins followed in Ygdrasil. Afterwards Mrs Hunkin called me Mrs Browning, which sounded so strange. And when we got back to the harbour everyone seemed to know what had happened, and were waving from houses and cottages. We quickly had breakfast, then loaded stores onto Yggy, and set off for the harbour mouth heading down-channel for the Helford river and Frenchman's Creek. We couldn't have chosen anything more beautiful.

The solitary yachtsman who leaves his yacht in the open roadstead of

Pont Creek. The sun shone on the day we married.

Helford, and goes exploring up-river in his dinghy on a night in midsummer, when the night-jars call, hesitates when he comes upon the mouth of the creek, for there is something of mystery about it even now, something of enchantment. Being a stranger, the yachtsman looks back over his shoulder to the safe yacht in the roadstead, and to the broad waters of the river, and he pauses, resting on his paddles, aware suddenly of the deep silence of the creek, of its narrow twisting channel, and he feels — for no reason known to him — that he is an interloper, a trespasser in time. He ventures a little way along the left bank of the creek, the sound of the blades upon the water seeming over-loud and echoing oddly among the trees on the farther bank, and as he creeps forward the creek narrows, the trees crowd yet more thickly to the water's edge, and he feels a spell upon him, fascinating, strange, a thing of queer excitement not fully understood.

He is alone, and yet — can that be a whisper, in the shallows, close to the bank, and does a figure stand there, the moonlight glinting upon his buckled shoes and that cutlass in his hand, and is that a woman by his side, a cloak around her shoulders, her dark ringlets drawn back behind her ears? He is wrong, of course, those are only the shadows of the trees, and the whispers are no more than the rustle of leaves and the stir of a sleeping bird, but he is baffled suddenly, and a little scared, he feels he must go no farther, and that the head of the creek beyond the farther bank is barred to him and must remain unvisited.

Frenchman's Creek is the only one of my novels that I am prepared to admit is romantic. A woman of means falls in love with a pirate — it sounds almost ridiculous! But there is more to it than that. Even today, if you sail the Helford during the magic moments before dusk falls, you can experience something of its mystery and

All the drowsy beauty of midsummer that gives Helford river a strange enchantment. We couldn't have chosen anything more beautiful.

'The creek, still and soundless, shrouded by trees, hidden from the eyes of men . . . This creek was a source of enchantment, a new escape, a place to drowse and sleep, a lotus-land.' *Frenchman's Creek*

enchantment. As you head down-river, the tide slackens, the trees darken, the birds are hushed, there is no sound except the whisper of water past the anchor chain until, if the yachtsman is lucky, he may yet hear the night-jar call. It is a summons unlike any other, churring, low, strangely compelling, so that on first hearing it you must think of neither bird nor beast but of some forgotten species, a scaly lizard cross-bred with a toad.

There is no sweetness here, no nightingale passion, no owl foreboding; the call is primitive, insistent, with a rhythmic rise and fall, coming not from the wooded slopes but from the open ground beyond, where amidst foxglove and gorse the night-jar crouches.

The title was not original: Q had used it many years before in one of his short stories, and graciously gave me permission to use it again, saying, if I remember rightly,

that he looked forward to seeing what I had made of it. In hindsight it seems less of a coincidence that Q 'touched' all three of the novels that speak of the primaeval spirit of Cornwall – *Jamaica Inn*, *Frenchman's Creek* and the novel on which we collaborated, *Castle Dor*, based upon the ancient Cornish legend of Tristan and Iseult.

These, more than any of my other novels, are about the mythic history, the mystery, the primaeval enchantment that make this land and its people what they are.

It was fourteen years after the death of Sir Arthur that his daughter Foy asked me to resolve and finish the manuscript of *Castle Dor*. He had begun to write it in the 1920s, a time when other writers invoked legend and mythology in their work – T S Eliot in *The Waste Land*, James Joyce in *Ulysses*. But whereas these writers used myths and legends – including that of Tristan – as a creative device to stimulate the imagination and to try to make sense of the modern world, Q maintained no such ironic distance.

He was a Cornishman through and through; for the Cornishman his legends are part of the reality of being Cornish, they are his inheritance. While I thought his novel worth preserving for its description of the Fowey countryside alone, it was his belief – that a soil once having brought to birth such a story of Tristan and

Iseult would be 'unable to forget or desist from the effort to throw up secondary shoots' – that convinced me.

The legend is one of seduction and betrayal. Mark (a king of Cornwall during the sixth century or possibly earlier), Iseult and Tristan form a triangle of jealous husband, faithless wife and ardent lover respectively, the two young people bent on deceit. Q intended a romance in his own Troy town between Linnet, the wife of an innkeeper, and Amyot, a Breton onion-seller; these two were meant to re-enact, in a more

St Winnow on the Fowey, where the lovers meet.

modern setting, the parts of Tristan and Iseult of ancient myth. One problem in resolving his novel was that its characters, like step-children, were not my own, their personalities were already formed. One character alone had my full sympathy, and this was Dr Carfax who, like Prospero, appeared to control events, and reminded me so much of Q himself.

The great Cornishman's close relationship with the country of his forefathers and his strong sense that myths and legends get at something universal – 'old, unhappy, far-off things' – about this ancient land, seem to place him in Carfax's position in the novel. For it is Carfax (a name derived from an old French word 'car-refures' meaning the place where all roads lead), who in some strange way sets in motion the whole story. In the prologue he stands under the stars at the historic hill fort of Castle Dor, waiting for the baby Linnet to be born to the blacksmith's wife. Imbued with the primaeval spirit of the site, as morning dawns, the good doctor seems about to discover the secret of this, the original Lancien, fortress-palace of King Mark, poised to mother once more its legendary tale of tragic love.

Castle an Dinas, where the climax of the novel, *Castle Dor*, takes place. 'It seemed to the doctor that he hovered on the threshold of another world.'

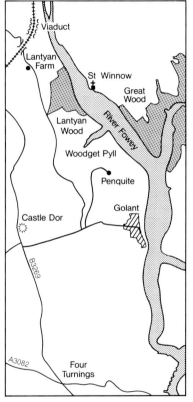

'How often Tommy and I (the search for Tristan constantly in mind) strolled beside Woodget Pyll and up to the lane above, beside Lantyan Woods, past Lantyan Farm and down to the further creek beneath the viaduct, and wondered whether one of the islands formed by the mud-flats in the creek when the tide withdraws, could have been the fighting ground of Tristan and Morholt.'

Four Turnings is the reputed burial site of Tristan; Castle Dor, the garrison fortress of King Mark; Lantyan farm, his palace; Woodget Pyll, known as Derrain Lake purportedly made by Mark for Iseult, his Queen, and stocked with swans, still seen today.

This most ancient cirque of Castle Dor, deserted, bramble-grown, was the very nipple of a huge breast in pain, aching for discharge.

Day broke slowly – closing a shutter on space to open another on time. For the rampart overlooks on the one hand a bay of the sea, on the other a river ford deep-set in a vale. From a nook of the bay, centuries ago, a soi-disant Caesar pushed out with his ships to win Rome. In a field sloping northward from the ramp, the guns and foot of a Parliament Army capitulated to King Charles on his last campaign of the West. The king had his coach anchored under the lee of a hedge yonder, and slept in it on the night before the surrender. Across the ford below regiments have stormed and shouted.

But these memories lifted themselves with the valley mists, to dissolve and trail away . . . and he knew that it was not for any secret of theirs he had been listening. All England is a palimpsest scored over with writ of love and hate, begettings of children beneath the hazels, betrayals, appeals, curses, concealed travails. But this was different somehow. It had no dimensions, small or great. In a way it had escaped dimensions, to be universal; and yet just here – here, waiting . . . An owl hooted up from the woods. A titlark on a stone announced the day. A moment later in the daylight the blacksmith, coming across the meadow, panted that all was well but he was wanted. Doctor Carfax closed his telescope, musing, and retraced his steps to the forge. The word, for a moment so close upon utterance, had escaped him.

Castle Dor, King Mark's ancient garrison fortress

CHAPTER THREE
The Calamity of Yesterday

When I first stayed at Ferryside I would seize every opportunity to explore, to walk for miles – bluebells everywhere – or cross the ferry to Fowey, walk through the town, and so to the castle on the cliff above the harbour mouth. Soon I discovered with fascination the enchanted woods on the Gribben headland, and one day looking north, inland from the Gribben, I could just make out the grey roof of a house set in its own grounds in the midst of the trees.

That would be Menabilly, I was told. Belongs to Dr Rashleigh, but he seldom lives there. Apparently the property had been first built in the reign of Queen Elizabeth, the grounds and woods had been in the last century famous for their beauty, and the property had never changed hands from the time it came into being, but had passed down, in the male line, to the present owner.

It was an afternoon in late autumn, the first time I tried to find the house. October, November, the month escapes me. But in the west country autumn can make herself a witch, and place a spell upon the walker.

We set forth, Angela and I, with a panting Pekinese held by a leash. We came to the lodge at Four Turnings, as we had been told, and opened the creaking iron gates with the flash courage and appearance of bluff common to the trespasser. The lodge was deserted. No one peered at us from the windows. We slunk away down the drive, and were soon hidden by the trees. I remember we did not talk, or if we did we talked in whispers. That was the first effect the woods had upon both of us.

The drive twisted and turned . . . it had the magic quality of a place hitherto untrodden, unexplored. I was Scott in the Antarctic. I was Cortez in Mexico. Or possibly I was none of these things, but a trespasser in time. The woods were sleeping now, but who, I wondered, had ridden through them once? What hoofbeats had sounded and then died away? What carriage wheels had rolled and vanished?

The trees grew taller and the shrubs more menacing. Yet still the drive led on, and never a house at the end of it. Suddenly Angela said, 'It's after four...and the sun's gone.' The Pekinese watched her, pink tongue lolling. And then he stared into the bushes, pricking his ears at nothing. The first owl hooted . . .

'I don't like it,' said Angela firmly. 'Let's go home.'

'But the house,' I said with longing, 'we haven't seen the house.'

Next morning I did a thing I had never done before . . . I rose at 5.00 am. I pulled across the harbour in my pram, walked through the sleeping town, and climbed out upon the cliffs just as the sun himself climbed out on Pont hill behind me.

She hesitated, and I dragged her on. But in an instant the day was gone from us. The drive was a muddied path, leading nowhere, and the shrubs, green no longer but a shrouding black, turned to fantastic shapes and sizes. There was not one owl now, but twenty. And through the dark trees, with a pale grin upon his face, came the first glimmer of the livid hunter's moon.

I knew then that I was beaten. For that night only.

We came back again to Cornwall in the following spring, and I was seized with a fever for fishing. I would be out in a boat most days, with a line in the water, and it did not matter much what came on the end of it, whether it would be seaweed or a dead crab, as long as I could sit on the thwart of a boat and hold a line and watch the sea. The boatman skulled off the little bay called Pridmouth, and as I looked at the land beyond, and saw the massive trees climbing from the valley to the hill, the shape of it all seemed familiar.

'What's up there, in the trees?' I said.

'That's Menabilly,' came the answer, 'but you can't see the house from the shore. It's away up yonder. I've never been there myself.' I felt a bite on my line at that moment and said no more. But the lure of Menabilly was upon me once again.

Next morning I did a thing I had never done before, nor ever did again, except once in the desert, where to see sunrise is the peak of all experience. In short, I rose at 5.00 am. I pulled across the harbour in my pram, walked through the sleeping town, and climbed out upon the cliffs just as the sun himself climbed out on Pont hill behind me. The sea was glass. The air was soft and misty warm. And the only other creature out of bed was a fisherman, hauling crab pots at the harbour mouth. It gave me a fine feeling of conceit, to be up before the world. My feet in sand shoes seemed like wings. I came down to Pridmouth bay, passing the solitary cottage by the lake, and, opening a small gate hard by, I saw a narrow path leading to the woods. Now, at last, I had the day before me, and no owls, no moon, no shadows could turn me back.

I followed the path to the summit of the hill and then, emerging from the woods, turned left, and found myself upon a high grass walk, with all the bay stretched out below me and the Gribben head beyond.

I paused, stung by the beauty of that first pink glow of sunrise on the water, but the path led on and I would not be deterred. Then I saw them for the first time – the scarlet rhododendrons. Massive and high they reared above my head, shielding the entrance to a long smooth lawn. I was hard upon it now, the place I sought. Some instinct made me crouch upon my belly and crawl softly to the wet grass at the foot of the shrubs. The morning

The only other creature out of bed was a fisherman, hauling crab pots at the harbour mouth.

mist was lifting, and the sun was coming up above the trees even as the moon had done last autumn. This time there was no owl, but blackbird, thrush and robin greeting the summer day.

I edged my way onto the lawn and there she stood. My house of secrets. My elusive Menabilly.

There she stood. My house of secrets. My elusive Menabilly . . .

The windows were shuttered fast, white and barred. Ivy covered the grey walls and threw tendrils round the windows. The house, like the world, was sleeping too. But later, when the sun was high, there would come no wreath of smoke from the chimneys. The shutters would not be thrown back, or the doors unfastened. No voices would sound within those darkened rooms. Menabilly would sleep on, like the sleeping beauty of the fairy tale, until someone should come to wake her.

As I sat on the edge of the lawn and stared at her I felt as many romantic, foolish people have felt about the Sphinx. Here was a block of stone, even as the desert Sphinx, made by man for his own purpose – yet she had a personality that was hers alone, without the touch of human hand. One family only had lived within her walls. One family who had given her life. They had been born there, they had loved, they had quarrelled, they had suffered, they had died. And out of those emotions she had woven a personality for herself, she had become what their thoughts and desires had made her.

Who can ever affirm or deny that the houses which have sheltered us as children, or as adults, and our predecessors too, do not have embedded in their walls, one with the dust and cobwebs, one with the overlay of fresh wallpaper and paint, the imprint of what-has-been?

Last night I dreamt I went to Manderley again. It seemed to me I stood by the iron gate leading to the drive, and for a while I could not enter, for the way was barred to me. There was a padlock and a chain upon the gate. I called in my dream to the lodge-keeper, and had no answer, and peering closer through the rusty spokes of the gate I saw that the lodge was uninhabited.

No smoke came from the chimney, and the little lattice windows gaped forlorn. Then, like all dreamers, I was possessed of a sudden

with supernatural powers and passed like a spirit through the barrier before me. The drive wound away in front of me, twisting and turning as it always had done, but as I advanced I was aware that a change had come upon it; it was narrow and unkept, not the drive that we had known. At first I was puzzled and did not understand, and it was only when I bent my head to avoid the low swinging branch of a tree that I realised what had happened. Nature had come into her own again and, little by little, in her stealthy, insidious way had encroached upon the drive with long, tenacious fingers. The woods, always a menace even in the past, had triumphed in the end . . .

On and on, now east now west, wound the poor thread that once had been our drive. Sometimes I thought it lost, but it appeared again, beneath a fallen tree perhaps, or struggling on the other side of a muddied ditch created by the winter rains. I had not thought the way so long. Surely the miles had multiplied, even as the trees had done, and this path lead but to a labyrinth, some choked wilderness and not to the house at all. I came upon it suddenly; the approach masked by the unnatural growth of a vast shrub that spread in all directions, and I stood, my heart thumping in my breast, the strange prick of tears behind my eyes.

There was Manderley, our Manderley, secretive and silent as it had always been, the grey stone shining in the moonlight of my dream, the mullioned windows reflecting the green lawns and the terrace. Time could not wreck the perfect symmetry of those walls, nor the site itself, a jewel in the hollow of a hand.

It is now more than fifty years since my novel, *Rebecca* (1938), was first published. The narrator, the 'I' of the story, is the companion to an elderly lady, Mrs Van Hopper. She is whisked away from their Mediterranean retreat, the Hotel Cote d'Azur, by Maxim de Winter, the owner of Manderley. She marries Maxim in the knowledge only that his first wife – Rebecca – was killed in a boating tragedy (and not that he had murdered her).

As the narrator nervously explores, Rebecca's powerful personality seems to radiate through the house. The west wing has been preserved by Mrs Danvers (the housekeeper), as it was in Rebecca's day, only shrouded in dust sheets, frozen in time. Rebecca is everywhere . . . in the arrangement and choice of furniture, in the candlesticks on the mantlepiece, in the pictures on the walls – 'little things, meaningless and stupid in themselves, but they were there for me to see, for me to hear, for me to feel. All had belonged to Rebecca. She had chosen them, they were not mine at all.'

Just as I had first come as a trespasser to Menabilly, so now 'I', the narrator, am made to feel the interloper, for Manderley is the sepulchral home of Rebecca's spirit and 'I' am but a trespasser in time.

In the woods at Menabilly with my three children, Tessa, Flavia, and Kits.

The beach at Pridmouth below Menabilly from which Rebecca goes to her death.

During the war, my husband and I were living in Hythe in Kent, but in 1943 changes of plans sent me to Cornwall with my three children. I had not visited Menabilly since the war began. No bombs had come her way, yet she looked like a blitzed building. The shutters were not shuttered now. The panes were broken. She had been left to die.

Left: Looking east from the Gribben towards Pridmouth.

It was easy to climb through the front windows. The house was stripped and bare. Dirty paper on the floor. Great fungus growths from the ceiling. I could scarcely see the soul of her for the despair. The mould was in her bones.

I returned to my furnished cottage, in angry obstinate mood. Something was dying, without hope of being saved. And I would not stand it. Yet there was nothing I could do. Nothing? There was one faint, ridiculous chance in a million . . . I telephoned my lawyer and asked him to write to the owner of Menabilly and ask him to let the house to me for a term of years. 'He won't consent for a moment,' I said. 'It's just a shot at random.'

But the shot went home . . . A week later my lawyer came to see me.

'By the way,' he said, 'I believe you will be able to rent Menabilly. But you must treat it as a whim, you know. The place is in a fearful state. I doubt if you could do more than camp out there occasionally.'

I stared at him in amazement. 'You mean – he would consent?' I said.

Something was dying, without hope of being saved. There was one faint, ridiculous chance in a million.

'Why, yes, I gather so,' answered my lawyer.

Then it began. Not the Battle of Britain, not the attack upon the soft underbelly of Europe that my husband was helping to conduct from Africa, but my own private war to live in Menabilly by the time winter came again . . .

'You're mad . . . you're crazy. . . you can't do it . . . there's no lighting . . . there's no water . . . there's no heating . . . you'll get no servants . . . it's impossible!'

The madness paid off. When Tommy came on leave for Christmas, expecting to find us squatting in camp beds with the rain pouring through the roof, he found the telephone installed, electric light in all the rooms, a hot bath waiting, and the furniture brought from store and put in just the places he would have chosen for himself. There were sprays of holly behind every picture. He grew to love it as much as I did, and forever after, during his lifetime, Christmas was always the high spot of the year.

And at midnight, when the children were asleep, and all was hushed and still, I would sit down at the piano and look at the panelled walls, and slowly, softly, with no one there to see, the house would whisper her secrets, and the secrets would turn to stories. In those days, in some eerie fashion, we became one, the house and I.

The first book that I wrote at Menabilly was *The King's General*, based on the memoirs of Honor Harris written just before she died in 1653, and largely concerning the period of the English Civil War. A tablet in her memory may still be seen to the right of the High Altar in nearby Tywardreath Church. Honor's memoirs combine with the events of the War and papers generously made available to me by the Rashleigh family, owners of Menabilly.

During the War some of the great Cornish estates changed hands as one family pitted itself against another. Jonathan Rashleigh, a supporter of the King, retained Menabilly but was ruined and his home destroyed, so that only the outer walls remained standing. In 1824 an extraordinary detail of Menabilly's history during these troubled years came to light when William Rashleigh had certain alterations made to the house, in the course of which the outer courtyard was removed, and blocked in to form kitchens and a larder.

The architect, summoned to do the work, noticed that the buttress against the north-west corner of the house served no useful purpose, and he told the masons to demolish it. This they proceeded to do, and on knocking

The madness paid off. When Tommy came on leave for Christmas . . . there were sprays of holly behind every picture. He grew to love it as much as I did.

away several of the stones they came upon a stair, leading to a small room, or cell, at the base of the buttress. Here thay found the skeleton of a young man, seated on a stool, a trencher at his feet, and the skeleton was dressed in the clothes of a Cavalier, as worn during the period of the Civil War. William Rashleigh, when he was told of the discovery, gave orders for the remains to be buried with great reverence in the churchyard at Tywardreath. And because he and his family were greatly shocked at the discovery, he ordered the masons to brick up the secret room, that no one in the household should come upon it in future. The alterations of the house continued, the courtyard was blocked in, a larder built against the buttress, and the exact whereabouts of the cell remained for ever a secret held by William Rashleigh and his architect.

This is how Honor Harris describes the cell in 1646: 'Six foot high, four square, it was not larger than a closet, and the stone walls, clammy cold with years, icy to my touch. There was a little stool against the corner, and by its side an empty trencher, with a wooden spoon. Cobwebs and mould were thick upon them . . .'

And the unfortunate Cavalier? William Rashleigh

The north-west corner of the house where, inside the buttress, they found the skeleton of a young man.

learnt that certain members of the Grenville family had hidden at Menabilly before the Cornish rising of 1648, and he surmised that one of them had taken refuge in the secret room and had been forgotten.

There are no more Grenvilles. One of the proudest and most famous families amongst the Cornish gentry is extinct in Cornwall, the name passing on to other branches east of the Tamar. Richard Grenville and his brother Bevil were key figures in the Royalist cause during the Civil War. Their grandfather, Sir Richard Grenville, had died holding off fifty-two Spanish galleons from the deck of his small ship 'Revenge'. Lionhearted courage was a quality inherited by both grandsons, but it was to Richard – the King's General of the novel – that the great man bequeathed his characteristic ruthlessness.

As they court secretly in the orchard of the Harris home at Lanrest, Honor surprises a gentleness in Richard and, 'too much in love to care a whit for anyone', they decide to get married. But when out hawking near the Grenville estate at Stowe in North Cornwall, Honor is thrown from her horse:

'Beware the chasm,' shouted Richard in my ear, pointing with his whip, but he was past me like the wind and I could not call to him.

The heron was now direct above my head, and the falcons lost to

At midnight, when the children were asleep and all was hushed, the house would whisper her secrets, and the secrets would turn to stories.

Looking across the moors to the sea from the Grenville Estate at Stowe in North Cornwall, where in *The King's General*, Honor Harris is thrown from her horse and crippled – '"Beware the chasm," Richard shouted in my ear.'

view, and I heard Gartred shout in triumph: 'They bind – they bind – my tiercel has her,' and, silhouetted against the sun, I saw one of the falcons locked against the heron and the two come swinging down to earth not twenty yards ahead.

I tried to swerve, but the mare had the mastery, and I shouted to Gartred as she passed me, 'Which way is the chasm?' but she did not answer me. On we flew towards the circle of stones, the sun blinding

my eyes, and out of the darkening sky fell the dying heron and the blood bespattered falcon, straight into the yawning crevice that opened out before me. I heard Richard shout, and a thousand voices singing in my ears as I fell.

It was thus, then, that I, Honor Harris of Lanrest, became a cripple, losing all power in my legs from that day forward . . . If anyone therefore thinks that a cripple makes an indifferent heroine to a tale, now is the time to close these pages and desist from reading. For you will never see me wed to the man I love, nor become the mother of his children. But you will learn how that love never faltered... and you will also learn how, for all my helplessness, I took the leading part in the drama that unfolded, my very immobility sharpening my senses and quickening my perception, while chance itself forced me to my role of judge and witness. The tale goes on, then – what you have read is just the prologue.

As in *Rebecca*, I identified strongly with the narrator. As the drama unfolds Honor Harris becomes an extension of the author, my persona in the past. And when the fate of the young Cavalier – Richard Grenville's son – is sealed, I feel the shadow of the buttress is upon both Honor and me. Sitting at my typewriter only yards from the site of the airless room I too hear 'the sound of a boy's voice calling my name in terror, of a boy's hand beating against the walls', and in the pitch-black night, I fancy I can see his ghost, 'vivid, terrible, accusing'. Then, like the crippled heroine of my novel, I feel constrained, frustrated at participating in the events of yesterday merely as 'judge and witness', an invalid of time.

The third of my novels set largely at Menabilly is *My Cousin Rachel*, motivated by the twin demons jealousy and suspicion. The novel turns on the way the past can re-surface in the present, and it does so in the novel by means of letters.

Letters set the tale in motion, they hint of conspiracy and act as an anchor of truth in the shifting sands of deception. But there are also letters that have never been sent or mislaid, which appear long after they have been written to haunt those who would write their own scripts of what-has-been for their own self-serving ends.

Philip Ashley and his guardian Ambrose live together at Menabilly in a kind of gentlemanly mysogyny through Philip's boyhood, adolescence and early manhood, and when Ambrose meets and marries Rachel on holiday in Italy, Philip feels an enormous sense of loss, and not a little jealous.

Later, Philip receives two letters from Ambrose, which appear to indicate that Rachel is poisoning him, and soon afterwards, Ambrose dies.

With characteristic, mock-heroic courage Philip adopts the role of investigator and travels to Italy to confront

'It was our highest point of land, saving the beacon to the south, and had a fine view over the woods and the valley to the open sea.' *My Cousin Rachel*

Rachel with the evidence of the letters. But when he arrives in Florence, Rachel has disappeared, and her smooth-talking adviser, Rainaldi does little to dispel the young man's suspicions. After his return to Cornwall, Rachel writes to Philip to ask whether she might bring home her late husband's effects and stay a while at Menabilly. Philip agrees but decides to act coldly towards her so that her stay will at least be as short as possible. However, within days of their meeting, Philip finds himself hopelessly in love with Rachel, and his infatuation consigns his suspicions to the back of his mind until one fine spring morning he is called to Sam Bate's house, the lodge on the east boundary of Menabilly. Sam has discovered a letter between the material and lining of a coat that had belonged to Ambrose and been handed on to the servant: 'It shook me, sir, to come upon it. It seemed, if you understand, as if I had come across a message from the dead.'

I did not return at once to the house. I climbed up through the woods to a path that runs above that part of the estate, bordering the Trennant acres and the wooded avenue. Ambrose had been fonder of this walk than any other. It was our highest point of land, saving the beacon to the south, and had a fine view over the woods and the valley to the open sea. The trees fringing the path, planted by Ambrose and his father before him, gave shelter, although not high enough as yet to dim the view, and in May month the bluebells made a cover to the ground. At the end of the path, topping the woods, before plunging to descent and the keeper's cottage in the gully, Ambrose had set up a piece of granite. 'This,' he said to me, half joking, half in earnest, 'can serve me for a tombstone when I die. Think of me here rather than in the family vault with the other Ashleys.'

I sat down beside the slab, and taking Ambrose's letter from my pocket placed it face downwards, on my knee. The red seal stared up at me, imprinted with his ring and the chough's head. The packet was not thick. It contained nothing. Nothing but a letter, which I did not want to open. I cannot say what misgiving held me back, what cowardly instinct drove me to hide my head like an ostrich in the sand. Ambrose was dead, and the past went with him when he died. I had my own life to make, and my own will to follow.

But not to read the letter . . . what would he say to that? If I tore it now to shreds, and scattered the pieces, and never learnt the contents, would he condemn me? I balanced the letter in my hand, this way and that. To read, or not to read; I wished to heaven the choice was not before me. Back in the house, my loyalty was with her. In the boudoir, with my eyes upon her face, watching those hands, that smile, hearing her voice, no letter would have haunted me. Yet

here, in the woods beside the slab of granite where we had so often stood together, he and I, Ambrose holding the very stick I carried now, wearing the same coat, here his power was strongest. Like a small boy who prays the weather will be fine upon his birthday I prayed to God now that the letter should contain nothing to disturb

'"This," he said to me, half joking, half in earnest, "can serve me for a tombstone when I die."

me, and so opened it. It was dated April of the preceeding year, and was therefore written three months before he died.

I have often been asked whether Rachel was really guilty of murdering Ambrose or whether it was in Philip's mind. I cannot answer the question. One moment I thought, 'Well, I wonder if she is?' and the next moment I was not at all sure. What is certain is that our past will not be buried, for it is alive, with us and within us. Philip's head-in-the-sand attitude serves only to expose the futility of trying to escape the hours and the days. Yesterday is not some milestone that has been passed in the journey of life, to be forgotten, buried. Like the ancient places and buildings around us, we are other than we were because of yesterday. And the past is intrinsic to our future, our destiny.

This, Philip will undoubtedly discover, for from the opening pages of *My Cousin Rachel*, the hangman's gibbet, which once stood at Four Turnings, is a kind of symbol of Philip's fate, insinuating, illuminating, rolling past, present and future into one. Four Turnings is the place where all roads meet, and where all strands of Philip's story seem to converge.

CHAPTER FOUR
Things Unknown

Walking down from Menabilly to the farm one day, I caught sight of the farmer on his tractor ploughing the fields, a cloud of screaming gulls circling above his head, and thought, 'Supposing the gulls attacked!' That picture started the brewing process for my short story, 'The Birds'.

The birds had been more restless than ever this fall of the year, the agitation more marked because the days were still. As the tractor traced its path up and down the western hills, the figure of the farmer silhouetted on the driving-seat, the whole machine and the man upon it would be lost momentarily in the great cloud of wheeling, crying birds. There were many more than usual, Nat was sure of this.

Always, in autumn, they followed the plough, but not in great flocks like those, nor with such clamour.

. . . It was that night the weather turned. Nat's bedroom faced east. He woke up just after two and heard the wind in his chimney. Not the storm and bluster of a sou'westerly gale, bringing the rain, but east wind, cold and dry. It sounded hollow in the chimney, and a loose slate rattled on the roof. Nat listened, and could hear the sea roaring in the bay. Even the air in the small bedroom had turned chill: a draught came under the skirting of the door, blowing upon the bed. Nat drew the blanket round him, lent closer to the back of his sleeping wife, and stayed wakeful, watchful, aware of misgiving without cause.

Then he heard the tapping on the window. There was no creeper on the cottage walls to break loose and scratch upon the pane. He listened, and the tapping continued until, irritated by the sound, Nat got out of his bed and went to the window. He opened it, and as he did so something brushed his hand, jabbing at his knuckles, grazing the skin. Then he saw the flutter of wings and it was gone, over the roof, behind the cottage.

In the story the gulls act as one body, bound together by some extra-ordinary power against a human prey so 'civilized' that few can understand, can recognise that in some sinister way the evolutionary tide has turned.

There is a faculty amongst the myriad threads of our inheritance that, unlike the chemicals in our bodies and in our brains, has not yet been pinpointed by science, or even fully examined. I like to call this faculty 'the sixth sense'. It is a sort of seeing, a sort of hearing, something between perception and intuition, an indefinable grasp of things unknown.

I've always been fascinated by psychic matters although I am not psychic myself – I've never met a ghost and don't care to contact 'the other world' or anything of that sort. But I do think there is something in what they call ESP, extra-sensory perception.

The phenomena of precognition, of telepathy, of dreaming true, all depend upon the sixth sense, and the therapeutic value of hypnosis, still in its infancy, depends upon it too. Latent in young children, animals and primitive peoples, and more highly developed in the East than in the West, this perceptual intuitive sense has long lain dormant in most civilized societies and is waiting to be tapped.

Many of my short stories, even the early ones like 'The Apple Tree', have a sort of psychic dimension. And of course the phenomenon appears in my story 'Don't Look Now', which became a wonderful film with Donald Sutherland and Julie Christie.

This extra source of power, this strange and sometimes mystical sense can sometimes act as guide, as mentor, warning us of danger, signalling caution, but it can also urge us to new discoveries and intuitions. Perhaps it explains my instinctual desire to uncover the past – a past often tantalizingly out of reach of our so-called normal senses. Certainly I believe the desire to belong both to the past and the present goes very deep in human nature, and it is an urge that strengthens when we get older.

My Grandpapa George developed the ability to 'visit' the past by dreaming true. He would lie back and in his mind's eye become the child he once was, and he wrote about this 'psychic' ability too. The happy memory of childhood was a memory he clung to all his life, and his wistful longing for what-was-once and cannot-be-again came to the surface in the written word when, in 1891, he published his first novel, *Peter Ibbetson*. It was enormously popular in its day and George became a very rich man.

My novel *The House on the Strand* owes a great debt to Grandpapa George and his *Peter Ibbetson*. I think he affected all of us children greatly. But its inspiration needed a vehicle, a storyline, which did not emerge until 1964, the year that Tommy and I realised that our lease at Menabilly was coming to an end and that we

My Grandpapa George developed the ability to 'visit' the past by dreaming true.

I moved to Kilmarth in June, 1969 . . . I would visit the empty house and walk round the rooms in a daze.

would have to look for another home.

The thought of moving from this particular bit of Cornwall was unbearable to both of us. But then like a miracle, the lease of the one-time dower house to Menabilly – Kilmarth – fell vacant, and it was only half a mile or so away, with a splendid view over the sea beloved so well.

Moving house after twenty-six years, is rather like facing a major operation. Especially if the house one leaves behind has been greatly loved. Also I felt sorry for the house; I was sure it would be melancholy without us.

There is a plant, the mandrake, which bleeds and shrieks when it is pulled up, and that is how I felt on leaving Menabilly. The feeling passed, but it was nearly ten years before I finally laid the ghost.

I moved to Kilmarth in June, 1969. Day by day, week by week, month by month, during the run-up period when we were planning what we hoped would be our final home, I would visit the empty house and walk

Ygdrasil, the little boat in which Tommy had come down to Fowey, sitting in the garden at Kilmarth.

The drawing room at Kilmarth, or long room as I call it, where I spend much of the day.

Kilmarth's splendid view over the sea, beloved so well.

round the rooms in a daze, trying to picture the sort of people who had lived in the house before. I found a lot of dusty bottles in a room in the basemant, bottles containing curious things like embryos. My predecessor had been a scientist, Professor Singer. I began to imagine what he got up to in this old house . . .

From an old man in the nearby village of Tywardreath I discover that the house dates back to the fourteenth century, and, from the County Record Office, that in 1327 one Roger Kylmerth owned it and that the foundations of his house are beneath me now.

So it was that I found the story line for *The House on the Strand*. It would be set both in the present and the past. Like Peter Ibbetson, its hero, Dick Young, would travel back in time, in this case to the fourteenth-century world of Roger Kylmerth. And he would do this not by dreaming true but by means of a drug prepared by his friend – a professor of biophysics named Magnus Lane – in the laboratory full of curious exhibits I found in the basement of Kilmarth, close to the foundations of Kylmerth's house.

I find the science of genetics, of which I knew little in my youth, exciting, even exhilarating. As an individual living here and now I am only too well aware that I possess feelings, emotions, a mind and body bequeathed to me by people long since dead who have made me what I am. Scientists are not prepared to acknowledge that a sixth sense capable of looking back into the past or forward to the future exists, or, when they do, they explain it in material terms, as a memory storehouse, connected to the brain, as Professor Lane does in a letter to Dick Young -

'Briefly, and in layman's language, the chemistry within the brain cells concerned with memory, everything we have done from infancy onwards, is reproducible, returnable, for want of a better term, in these same cells, the exact content of which depends on our hereditary make-up, the legacy of parents, grandparents, remoter ancestors back to primaeval times. The fact that I am a genius and you are a lay-about depends soley on the messages transmitted to us from these cells and then distributed through the various other cells and throughout our body, but our various characteristics apart, the particular cells I have been working upon – which I will call the memory-box – store not only our memories but habits of the earlier brain pattern we inherit. These habits, if released to consciousness, would enable us to see, hear, become cognoscent of things that happened in the past, not because any particular ancestor witnessed any particular scene, but because with the use of a medium – in this

I discover that in 1327 one Roger Kylmerth owned the site and that the foundations of his house are beneath me now . . . So it was that I found the story line for *The House on the Strand*.

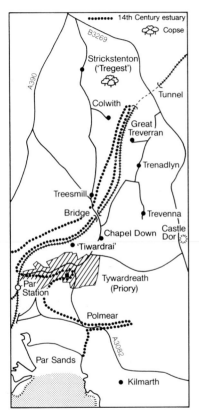

This is the country of The House on the Strand. *Kilmarth was built on the the foundations of Roger Kylmerth's 14th-century house. The walk down Polmear hill and on to Tywardreath church is Dick Young's first adventure into the past, the dotted lines show the reach of the sea 600 years ago. Chapel Down (now the name of a Bungalow), Treesmill and the railway bridge are clues to Dick's search for Tiwardrai, the house on the strand itself. Further north the place names lead the detective lost in time to Tregest, the house of beautiful Isolda Carminowe, unless of course there happens to be a train passing through the tunnel north of Treverran.*

case a drug – the inherited, older brain pattern takes over and becomes dominant.'

There is no cell in our bodies that has not been transmitted to us by our ancestors . . . We are all of us chemical particles, inherited not only from our parents but from a million ancestors. Our past is virtually limitless.

For this reason alone none of us is isolated in time, a mere expression of the present. In a very real sense, 'yesterday is within us'. We are part of what we were once and of what we are yet to become in successive generations.

But for me the novel would be more than an exploration of the logical possibilities of genetic theory. Dick's travels back into the past are mine, the writer's. We have walked together, Dick and I, about that other world 'with a dreamer's freedom but with a waking man's perception'. I share with him the empathy that he feels with the lives of his fourteenth-century characters because it is so similar to how I felt when writing about the people who had built and sailed 'Jane Slade', or the people who had lived and died once at Menabilly. 'Intense involvement but intense compassion too. Yes, that was the word, compassion. And I had no way of explaining my sense of participation in all they did,

Tywardreath. The hill by the church where, in the 14th Century, the sea came in (see map).

unless it was that stepping backwards out of my time to theirs, I felt them vulnerable, and more certainly doomed to die than I was myself, knowing indeed, that they had been dust for more than six centuries.'

Here, Dick describes his first experience of the drug.

The first thing I noticed was the clarity of the air, and then the sharp green colour of the land. There was no softness anywhere. The distant hills did not blend into the sky but stood out like rocks, so close that I could almost touch them, their proximity giving me a shock of surprise and wonder which a child feels looking for the first time through a telescope. Nearer to me, too, each object had the same hard quality, the very grass turning to single blades, springing from a younger, harsher soil than the soil I knew.

I had expected – if I expected anything – a transformation of another kind: a tranquil sense of well-being, the blurred intoxication of a dream, with everything about me misty, ill-defined; not this tremendous impact, a reality more vivid than anything hitherto experienced, sleeping or awake. Now every impression was heightened, every part of me singularly aware: eyesight, hearing, sense of smell, all had been in some way sharpened . . .

I was walking downhill towards the sea, across those fields of sharp-edged silver grass that glistened under the sun, for the sky –

dull, a moment ago, to my ordinary eyes – was now cloudless, a blazing ecstatic blue. I remembered that the tide had been out, the stretches of flat sand exposed, the row of bathing-huts, lined like dentures in an open mouth, forming a solid background to the golden expanse. Now they had gone, and with them the rows of houses fronting the road, the docks, all of Par – chimneys, rooftops, buildings – and the sprawling tentacles of St Austell enveloping the countryside beyond the bay. There was nothing left but grass and scrub, and the high distant hills that seemed so near; while before me the sea rolled into the bay, covering the whole stretch of sand as if a tidal wave had swept over the land, swallowing it in one rapacious draught. To the north-west, the cliffs came down to meet the sea, which, narrowing gradually, formed a wide estuary, the waters sweeping inward, following the curve of the land and so vanishing out of sight.

When I came to the edge of the cliff and looked beneath me, where the road should be, the inn, the café, the almshouses at the base of Polmear hill, I realised that the sea swept inland here as well, forming a creek that cut to the east, into the valley. Road and houses had gone, leaving only a dip between the land which rose on either side of the creek . . . I descended the hill and stood beside the creek . . .

I drank deep of the cold air, filling my lungs. Just to breathe was a joy never yet experienced for its own sake, having some quality of

The church at Tywardreath, where Dick is led by Roger Kylmerth and his adventures in the 14th Century begin.

The site of the de Champernounes' manor house – Tiwardrai, that Dick Young discovers on his trip into the past.

Kilmarth is not the house on the strand, though it is often assumed to have been by people who have not read the novel. It is of course Tiwardrai, as shown on the map. The 14th century background to the novel is all carefully researched. Tiwardrai means 'house on the strand' and is mentioned in Domesday.

Par beach. 'There was nothing left but grass and scrub, and the high distant hills that seemed so near.'

magic that I had not sensed before. Impossible to analyse thought, impossible to let my reason play on what I saw: in this new world of perception and delight there was nothing but intensity of feeling to serve as guide.

I might have stood forever, entranced, content to hover between earth and sky, remote from any life I knew or cared to know; but then I turned my head and saw that I was not alone. The hoofs had made no sound – the pony must have travelled as I had done, across the fields – and now that it trod upon the shingle the clink of stone against metal came to my ears with a sudden shock, and I could smell the warm horse-flesh, sweaty and strong.

Instinct made me back away, startled, for the rider came straight towards me, unconscious of my presence.

Dick becomes obsessed with the motivations and injustices of the people and plots he uncovers in the other world, and, like the writer of his story, he thrills to the excavating of the past:

Roger Kylmerth had been no faded snapshot in time's album; and even now, in this fourth dimension into which I had stumbled, he lived and moved, ate and slept, beneath me in his house, Kylmerth, enacting his living Now which ran side by side with my immediate Present... There was no past, no present, no future. Everything living is part of the whole. We are all bound, one to the other, through time and eternity, and, our senses once opened, as mine have been opened

by the drug, to a new understanding of his world and mine, fusion would take place, there would be no separation, there would be no death... To me it proved that the past was living still, that we are all participants, all witnesses. I was Roger, I was Bodrugan, I was Cain; and in being so was more truly myself.

The whereabouts of Tregest, the house of the beautiful Isolda Carminowe (Strickstenton on today's map), is the final piece in the 600-year-old jigsaw that Dick and Professor Lane are determined to finish. Lane, encouraged by Dick's reports of his drug's effects, takes a dose himself and sets out to find Tregest. North of Great Treverran he meets his death when a passing freight train intrudes upon the 14th-century world.

The quest absorbs both Magnus and Dick, as completely as the imaginary characters and plots absorb me when I sit in front of my typewriter and a story unfolds. But at length Dick falls victim to his illusions, as anyone must who seeks to attach undue significance to perceptions that in this world can be no more (nor less) than hieroglyphics – the words of a novelist on a page. For in truth, time defines human existence. Only our mortality offers us the promise of our beliefs and intuitions. Perhaps that is the great irony of the death we all so fear.

> *Last night the other world came much too near,*
> > *And with it fear.*
> *I heard their voices whisper me from sleep,*
> > *And could not keep*
> *My mind upon the dream, for still they came,*
> > *Calling my name,*
> *The loathly keepers of the netherland*
> > *I understand.*
> *My frozen brain rejects the pulsing beat;*
> > *My willing feet,*
> *Cloven like theirs, too swiftly recognise*
> > *Without surprise.*
> *The horn that echoes from the further hill,*
> *Discordant, shrill,*
> *Has such a leaping urgency of song,*
> > *Too loud, too long,*
> *That prayer is stifled like a single note*
> > *In the parched throat.*
> *How fierce the flame! How beautiful and bright*
> > *The inner light*
> *Of that great world which lives within our own,*
> > *Remote, alone.*
> *Let me not see too soon, let me not know,*
> > *And so forgo*
> *All that I cling to here, the safety side*
> > *Where I would bide.*
> *Old Evil, loose my chains and let me rest*
> > *Where I am best,*
> *Here in the muted shade of my own dust.*
> > *But if I must*
> *Go wandering in Time and seek the source*
> > *Of my life force,*
> *Lend me your sable wings, that as I fall*
> > *Beyond recall,*
> *The sober stars may tumble in my wake,*
> > *For Jesus' sake.*
> > > *'Another World'*

Epilogue

I still love walking on my own; it's become a sort of ritual. I go out over the cliffs and down the beach where I used to swim, and then back again. It's not lonely, it's just that I've always liked being on my own. If I had to choose something to do, I think I'd be a shepherd on the mountains in Crete, standing, leaning upon a staff and pottering with the sheep.

I have an awful feeling that the spirit of Cornwall is changing, the quietude, the solitude of it all. In the final chapter of *Vanishing Cornwall*, which I wrote twenty-two years ago now, I ask the question, 'What does the future hold for Cornwall?' Will it indeed become the playground of all England, chalets and holiday camps set close to every headland, despite the efforts of the country planning authorities and the National Trust to preserve the coast?

I provided a sort of answer in my last novel, *Rule Britannia*. At that time, in the early seventies, there was an awful lot going on in Northern Ireland, people resenting the army, and I thought how Cornwall would do if suddenly friendly soldiers, like the Americans, landed. Who would resist and who collaborate? So in the novel Cornwall is invaded not by tourists but by the American army. A new USUK alliance has been formed in the wake of economic disaster, and the Americans have a clear idea about where the remedy lies.

Plans for Great Britain herself would take some little time to formulate. It must be recognised that her heyday as a great industrial nation had now ended, but a new future lay ahead for her as the historical and cultural centre of the English-speaking peoples. Just as some years previously people on holiday had gone in their thousands to the Costa Brava in Spain for sea and sunshine, so now tourists would flock in their millions to explore the country that had given birth to Shakespeare, Milton, Lord Byron . . .

'Don't you see,' said Martha Hubbard, 'that what you have to sell here in the UK is not sunshine or bathing beaches, but historical background. Why, the whole of the west coast from north Wales down to Cornwall here can be developed as one vast leisure-land. With the good Welsh folk dressed in their costumes, tall hats and cloaks, serving potato-cakes to the tourists from the States, they wouldn't be talking any more of unemployment. The same in Cornwall. Now, we in the States don't need to purchase your clay, but construct a miniature Switzerland out of your white mountains and train your unemployed as ski instuctors and sleigh-drivers...'

It was Fortress Cornwall a decade before the Falklands, but I fear that the plans for exploiting our heritage may have been just as prophetic. A lot of people who think of me as a recluse, shut away in a remote house on the cliffs in Cornwall, identify me with Mad in Rule Britannia. She's the rather left-wing, eccentric actress who dresses in an outfit reminiscent of 'the uniform worn by the late lamented Mao Tse-tung', lives in a house like mine overlooking the bay, and has no intention of letting the Americans have their way.

I don't mind that, if the same people also attribute something of Mad's spirit of resistance to me. I'm sure my grandchildren would. While the story was brewing the young Browning boys spent their summer holidays here at Kilmarth, rushing about the woods, playing with their Action Men. As an old girl, past her prime, I could hardly join in their war games. But I was the first to encourage 'An Attack' on the ruined cottage in the shrubbery! And would secretly watch from the window whilst these daily battles raged in the summer sun.

A lot of myself did indeed go into the character of Mad, and sometimes it's very easy to think of Kilmarth as an outpost, a last frontier. And how appropriate, for shortly before moving here I discovered that the word 'Kilmarth' in Cornish means 'Retreat of Mark'. Perhaps this site was also the last outpost of the aged Cornish king (King Mark of the Tristan legend) who, with passion spent and jealousy forgotten, came, like me, to rest and look out in peace across the sea.

Daphne du maurier

Afterword

I heard the old, old men say,
'Everything alters,
And one by one we drop away.'
They had hands like claws, and
their knees
Were twisted like the old
thorn-trees
By the waters.
I heard the old, old men say,
'All that's beautiful drifts away
Like the waters.'

W B Yeats

I heard an old man once say that when we die in our homes, the windows should be opened wide, that the soul within our earthly body can fly out and escape to the hereafter or whatever awaits us on the other side.

On April 19th, 1989, a little after eight in the morning, my mother's dedicated nurse went in to wake her, only to find that she had past peacefully away in her sleep. She knew of the old saying and immediately threw open the windows. She told me later she thought the soul circled round the house, as if to make a last triumphant orbit, before flying out across the sweep of Par bay.

I took great comfort from hearing this, for during my mother's lifetime, the sea had always been one of her great loves and would surely play some part in her eternity. She had a vision of my father standing proudly on deck of his small motor boat at the entrance of Fowey Harbour, his arms held out in welcome. The sea was calm and the light dazzling from a setting sun. Here, she would join him, and they would sail away to wherever awaited them. A child-like perception of heaven if you like, but as we near our end in old age, it would seem our minds can revert to simple, trusting beliefs which we held when very young. Perhaps to recapture that long lost innocence with which we were born.

I remember in her last years how my mother became fascinated with pictures and photographs of her forbears who adorned the walls and tables of her home. She would hold lovingly a picture of a dear dead granny to her, or kiss the photograph of an adored uncle killed in the First War. We had been brought up with these same faces, staring at us from their well-worn frames, and she had passed them off with distracted affection. Now, in her old age, these same familiar faces became more real, and were looked upon with new-found fondness.

Tregaminion Church, situated between Kilmarth and Menabilly.

It was of course her love for Cornwall and the three houses that she lived in at various times between 1928 and 1989 that really meant most to her. Ferryside, at Bodinnick, opposite Fowey, where she wrote her first novel, *The Loving Spirit*, and where she met my father and fell in love. It was here that she found what she called 'her freedom'. A freedom that enabled her to write, to explore, to learn to sail, to find her true self. Over sixty years later, looking across the harbour from Fowey, it is easy to see why Ferryside bewitched her and she remembered a line from a forgotten book, where a lover looks for the first time upon his chosen one – 'I for this, and this for me.'

So to Menabilly where she stayed for twenty-six years. Her house of secrets and the inspiration for so much of her writing. A home for us children in which to grow up and play in an idyllic never-never land. Summers seemed to last for ever and the sun always shone, and the sea was always warm. But childhood memories are deceiving. Forgotten are the freezing winters, the burst pipes and the trees dripping endlessly after days of lashing rain. What I will not forget was the dark at the top of the stairs and the long passage that led to the old disused part of the house. I never saw a phantom shape but I feel certain there was something nasty, unexplained, lurking in the deep shadows! The house was returned to the Rashleigh family in 1969, and the du Maurier enthusiast who travels to Cornwall in search of Manderley and tries to gain access to Menabilly will be disappointed. But they should remember that it is a private house and respect the wishes of the present owner, whose forbears have owned it for centuries.

Finally, my mother rented another property belonging to the Rashleigh family, Kilmarth, a couple of miles from her former home. It was a lovely, open house, filled with sunlight, and my wife and I spent many happy summer holidays there with our four children. My mother grew to accept the move from Menabilly. She was soon to feel, as she put it, 'at one with the house'. She was at home.

It was here that she wrote her last great novel, *The House on the Strand*. Once again, it was the house that inspired the story. By continuing with her writing she was able to over come the profound disappointment that my father, who had died in 1965, could not be with her in her last home. She was never happier than when she was writing. She enjoyed the discipline, especially that which she imposed upon herself for her short stories. 'The Birds' and 'Don't Look Now' are probably the best known and became successful films. In the mid-1980s, alas, her fertile imagination began to desert her and the

Ferryside today.

inspiration to write faded. We all visited her frequently but her last years were sad ones. Without the power of creativity, she felt life was meaningless.

After my mother's death we held a private memorial service at Tregaminion church, which is situated between Kilmarth and Menabilly. Later, my sisters and I scattered her ashes over her chosen spot above the cliffs. The sea below was calm, sheltered from the east wind, and a pale, hesitant sun tried to break through the clouds. Somewhere, a seagull cried across the bay, and then a shaft of sunlight appeared on the water and I was reminded of an old friend's poem, 'The Light under the Sea', and how mother would say it was the Spirit moving upon the waters, and that it was always a good omen.

Kilmarth was empty for several years but has now been sold and I hope it will be a happy home again and that laughter and music will flood across the lawn once more. In 1993, my wife and I were fortunate enough to purchase Ferryside from my aunt, Angela du Maurier, who was in poor health. It is a dream house and I trust that if my mother were to look down upon us, she would be delighted that we are now living in the house that first drew her to Cornwall and bewitched her with its enchantment.

Christian Browning, 1995

Books by Daphne du Maurier

The Loving Spirit, *Heinemann 1931*
I'll Never Be Young Again, *Heinemann 1932*
Julius, *Heinemann 1933*
Gerald: a Portrait, *Gollancz 1934*
Jamaica Inn, *Gollancz 1936*
The Du Mauriers, *Gollancz 1937*
Rebecca, *Gollancz 1938*
Come Wind, Come Weather, *Heinemann 1940*
Frenchman's Creek, *Gollancz 1941*
Hungry Hill, *Gollancz 1943*
The Years Between (play), *Gollancz 1945*
The King's General, *Gollancz 1946*
September Tide (play), *Gollancz 1949*
The Parasites, *Gollancz 1949*
The Young George du Maurier: A selection of his Letters, 1860-1870 (Ed.) *Peter Davies 1951*
My Cousin Rachel, *Gollancz 1951*
The Apple Tree, *Gollancz 1952*
Happy Christmas, *Todd 1953*
Mary Anne, *Gollancz 1954*

Early Stories, *Todd 1955*
The Scapegoat, *Gollancz 1957*
The Breaking Point, *Gollancz 1959*
The Infernal World of Branwell Brontë, *Gollancz 1960*
Castle Dor, *J M Dent 1962*
The Glass Blowers, *Gollancz 1963*
The Flight of the Falcon, *Gollancz 1965*
Vanishing Cornwall, *Gollancz 1967*
The House on the Strand, *Gollancz 1969*
Not After Midnight, *Gollancz 1971*
Rule Britannia, *Gollancz 1972*
Golden Lads: Anthony Bacon, Francis and their Friends, *Gollancz 1975*
The Winding Stair: Francis Bacon, His Rise and Fall, *Gollancz 1976*
Echoes from the Macabre, *Gollancz 1976*
Myself When Young, *Gollancz (as Growing Pains: the Shaping of a Writer) 1977*
The Rendezvous and Other Stories, *Gollancz 1980*
The Rebecca Notebook and Other Memories, *Gollancz 1981*
Classics from the Macabre, *Gollancz 1987*
Enchanted Cornwall, *Pilot/Michael Joseph 1989*

Index